More Stories to Draw

by
Jerry J. Mallett
and
Timothy S. Ervin

Published by Alleyside Press, a Division of Freline, Inc.
P.O. Box 889
Hagerstown, Maryland 21741

ISBN 0-913853-11-9

Printed in the United States of America

Contents

About Storytelling

The Value of Storytelling

People the world over have always been fascinated by stories. In earlier centuries, storytelling was a valuable social skill. The storyteller enjoyed considerable prestige and was depended on for entertainment, relaxation, and enlightenment.

Learning the ancient art of storytelling is well worth the effort for the pleasure it affords both the teller *and* the audience. When the librarian or teacher uses storytelling in the library or classroom, the students are directly and intimately involved with the story. Storytelling allows the teller to move around, use gestures and eye contact, clown a bit, and even involve the listeners as characters in the story. These things can make stories come alive for listeners.

Storytelling also helps children become familiar with the story language and story structures. Familiarity with these aspects helps them read stories themselves more easily and enjoy them more. It also helps in introducing them to the plots and themes that run through all literature.

In addition, storytelling provides the stimulus for children's storytelling. Seeing the librarian or teacher engage in storytelling helps children understand that storytelling is a worthy activity, and motivates them to tell their own stories.

Choosing the Story

The most important factor in choosing a story is to select one that is really *enjoyable*. The narrator should enjoy spending time preparing the story and retelling it with conviction and enthusiasm. It must also fit the narrator's personality, style, and talents. This is important because whatever pleasure the narrator derives from telling the story is conveyed to the children.

Storytelling demands an appreciative audience. Therefore, the selected story must also be *appropriate* for the listeners. The storyteller must be aware of children's interests, ages, and experience. Young children have short attention spans, so story length must be considered when selecting a tale. Children's ages will also influence the subject matter of the tale. Young children like stories about familiar subjects such as animals, children, or home life. They respond to the repetitive language in cumulative tales and enjoy joining in when appropriate. Children from roughly ages seven through ten enjoy folktales with longer plots. Older children enjoy adventure tales, myths, and legends.

Whatever the choice, the storyteller must *feel at ease* with the material, must *enjoy* the story, and must want to *share* it with others.

Preparing the Story for Telling

Storytelling does not require memorization, but it does require preparation. Certain steps will help the storyteller prepare for this enjoyable experience.

First, divide the story into units of action—that is, identify the major events of the plot. If you strip away the descriptive material, most stories easily divide into definable series of actions.

The second step is to identify any recurring phrases or refrains that need to be memorized. For example, in *Jack and the Beanstalk* the giant consistently declares, "Fee Fi Fo Fum, I smell the blood of an Englishman." This needs to be told exactly as it appears in the story in order to retain the spirit of the tale.

The third step is to practice telling the story until you feel at ease and are sure you will remember it. It is advisable to use a tape recorder to evaluate your presentation for pitch, enunciation, timing, and expression.

Chalk Talks or Drawing Stories

This book, *More Stories to Draw*, highlights a special storytelling technique, that of the "chalk talk." This popular type of story is unique in that the development of the plot coincides with the development of a picture that is completed as the story ends. Older children try to guess the pictorial conclusion beforehand, with the aid of the clues given within the context of the story and the partially completed drawing. But younger children are often quite surprised when they see the finished picture. Either way results in a lot of fun for everyone involved! Good chalk talks all have the elements of surprise and suspense and present a challenge for children at any level.

The belief that the presentation of such a story is difficult for those without a lot of artistic talent is wrong, for these stories entail only simple line drawings. Even if the narrator has minimal artistic talent, he can achieve immediate and gratifying success when using a chalk talk.

Knowing what the completed drawing will look like is a tremendous help for remembering the story sequence. Often, starting with the finished drawing and working backwards is helpful. Having the entire drawing to work with is immensely useful in the first learning step.

A story's sequence of action is revealed on the chalkboard through connecting lines and shapes that develop toward the culmination of the story. The finished drawing makes the point of the story—often in a surprising or humorous way. The use of such a visual aid has the added feature of acting as an attention-holder for the audience.

Here Comes Dad

Bobby Jo lived about as far out in the country as you could get. At least that's what he thought. Nobody but *nobody* ever passed their old farmhouse! The only way you could get to Bobby Jo's farmhouse was to take a dirt road off the main highway.

Whenever his mother and father would go into town, they would always take Bobby Jo with them. He always liked going, but it was the coming home trip that seemed to take forever. The only part of the trip that interested him was the ride over the old Talmadge Bridge. It was A LONG BRIDGE that was high over the Maumee River.

THE MOON was full that night . . .

. . . and so Bobby Jo could easily see the Maumee River far below him. The moon shone on the river and seemed to highlight EVERY WAVE as the car sped across the bridge.

As soon as they were across the river, the highway CIRCLED around a large mountain . . .

. . . and then came to THE CROSSROADS where Bobby Jo's family would turn.

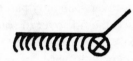

From this point on, THE ROAD WAS NOTHING BUT DIRT, and they wouldn't pass another farmhouse . . .

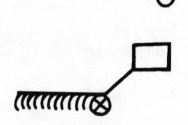

. . . until they finally came to THEIR OWN HOUSE, where the road ended.

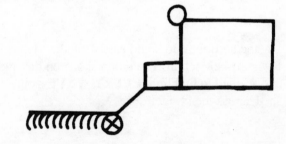

Bobby Jo went right to bed and slept soundly, since he had had a very busy day in town. In fact, he didn't wake up until his mother called, "Bobby Jo . . . you sleepyhead . . . get out of bed. Do you want to sleep all day long?"

Bobby Jo jumped out of bed. The sun was beaming into his bedroom. He rushed over to the window and looked out. Off to the side of the house was THE BIG OLD BARN.

Some of THE PAINT WAS PEELING OFF the upper corner and he giggled to himself. His dad had said he was going to paint that old barn so many times that his mother would just shake her head and say, "Sam, that old barn will fall down all around us before you paint it."

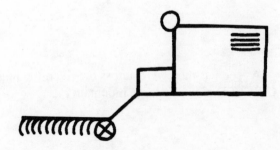

Behind the barn stood THE SILO that was always empty now that Dad took their corn to the grain elevator in town.

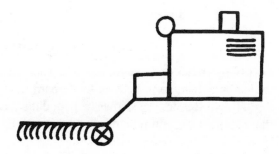

As Bobby Jo was looking at the silo, A LARGE FLOCK OF BIRDS flew over it.

"I bet you're going to your favorite place," thought Bobby Jo.

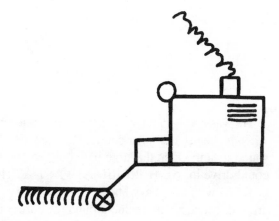

He watched as they circled over THE LARGE LAKE in back of their house . . .

. . . and then flew down to THE ISLAND in the middle of the lake. "Just as I thought," he said knowingly.

"Bobby Jo," called his mother, "You have your chores to do. Now get a move on."

Bobby Jo hurried and got dressed. Then, after a quick breakfast, he rushed out to the barn.

"Hi, old Bessie," he said as he patted the cow on her rump. "I bet you're hungry and thirsty." He grabbed a large bucket, went out the side door, and WALKED DOWN TO THE WELL.

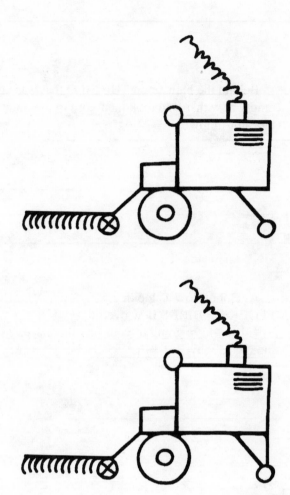

He was about to return with the filled bucket when he heard a familiar sound. He knew what the sound meant: Open the large barn door so his dad could drive in. HE HURRIED AS FAST AS HE COULD with the heavy bucket of water and arrived just as his dad came around the corner of the barn.

Now what do you suppose his dad was riding?

It's a Bird! It's a Plane! It's Vladmere!

Vladmere was just like any other bird—or so he thought. He really wasn't a bird at all. But neither Vladmere nor his friends SPECK AND TINY knew that. They thought they were all sparrows!

All three lived in an old empty barn and spent every morning making flight patterns high in the rafters. The only trouble was that while Speck and Tiny would make FIGURE EIGHTS, Vladmere would fly in CIRCLES.

"The sun's too bright," Vladmere would say. "I can't see very well."

Still, the three played well together, chasing each other through the barn. THEY WOULD WEAVE IN AND OUT OF THE MASSIVE BEAMS.

"Time for Tag," said Speck.

Tiny was "it" and Vladmere and Speck began chasing Tiny AROUND THE BALES OF HAY.

Tiny would RACE OUT OF THE DOOR
AND SPECK WOULD FOLLOW.

Vladmere would try to follow but he usually
WENT THE WRONG WAY.

"The sun," sighed Tiny and Speck.

One day, Vladmere had gone the wrong way
one too many times.

"I give up!" he cried, and he FLEW UP into
the rafters.

Speck was worried. Tiny said they should let
him cool off before talking with him.

That night, right before bed, Tiny and Speck flew up to where Vladmere had gone to sulk. They couldn't believe their eyes. Sound asleep, with his EARS POINTING TO THE GROUND . . .

. . . and his WINGS POINTING TO THE ROOF was Vladmere.

SPECK AND TINY looked at each other and smiled. Now they knew the reason why Vladmere couldn't play well during the day. He wasn't a bird at all.

What was Vladmere?

Who's at the Door?

Robbie and Rebecca were playing a game in Robbie's bedroom when they heard a faint scratching sound.

"What is that sound?" asked Rebecca.

"I don't know," answered Robbie, and he went to look out of THE SMALL ROUND WINDOW in his room.

Then they heard the sound again.

"Maybe we should go see what it is," said Rebecca.

So the brother and sister WALKED OUT OF ROBBIE'S ROOM . . .

. . . and DOWN THE UPSTAIRS HALLWAY.

It was getting dark outside and so they turned on THE HALLWAY LIGHT . . .

. . . before going DOWN THE STAIRWAY.

"I think the sound came from the back door," said Rebecca, and she began WALKING IN THAT DIRECTION.

Just then they heard the scratching sound again.
"No," said Robbie, "it's coming from the *front* door."
So the children WALKED BACK TO THE FRONT HALLWAY.

"I sure wish Mom and Dad were home," said Rebecca.
"Me too," added Robbie as they slowly MADE THEIR WAY TO THE FRONT DOOR.

When they reached THE FRONT DOOR . . .

. . . Robbie said, "gosh, look at those beetles."
"Yuk," added Rebecca.
There were FOUR BIG BLACK BEETLES on
their door.
"So *that's* what the scratching is!" said Rebecca.
"Shoo!" said Robbie as he made a waving motion
at the beetles.

Two of the beetles FLEW AWAY . . .

. . . and the other two RAN ACROSS THE FLOOR.

"There," said Robbie, quite satisfied with himself.

Just then the scratching again sounded at the front door.

"Oh no," said Rebecca. "Maybe we ought to open the door and see what's there!"

"Let me look out of the keyhole first," said Robbie.

When he looked out of the keyhole, he said, "Oh gosh, there is another EYE LOOKING BACK AT ME!"

Just then they heard their parents' CAR COMING UP THE DRIVEWAY.

A sigh of relief came over the two children.

"Now we can open the door," said Robbie bravely as he took the key OUT OF HIS POCKET.

What do you think the children found when they opened the front door?

A Girl's Best Friend

Yuk! It was cold, dark, rainy, and just plain miserable on Tuesday morning. But at six o'clock Sharla turned off her alarm, slowly crawled out of bed, and began dressing. This was the part about having Dot she didn't like. She did it, mind you. But she didn't *like* it. She CREPT DOWN THE STAIRS . . .

. . . and out the back door. She went AROUND THE CORNER of the house to the barn.

She PULLED OPEN the barn doors quickly to get out of the cold damp morning.

Silently she FLICKED ON the bright,
warm light.

Once the barn was well-lit, she started
toward the OTHER END, where Dot's food
was kept.

She put what she needed in the wagon and
pulled it back slowly to the front of the barn
as loose bits of HAY FELL OFF the wagon.

After she stopped the wagon, she got A WATER BUCKET . . .

. . . and filled it from THE HOSE with clean, clear, icy water.

Shivering all the way, she grabbed an empty coffee can and WENT TO THE GRAIN BIN to fill it with grain.

Thinking that the more quickly she moved, the warmer she would stay, she ran to Dot and PUT THE WATER BUCKET DOWN.

Then she SPRINKLED THE GRAIN on top of the hay.

As soon as the last piece of grain fell upon the hay, Dot STRETCHED HIS LONG NECK AROUND his stall door. It was almost as if he was thanking Sharla.

Sharla then knew that having a friend like Dot was worth any trouble on any morning.

What kind of friend was Dot?

Old Jake

His real name was John Brewster, but just about nobody remembered it. He had been called Old Jake for so long that no one would have known him by any other name. He lived in A SMALL HOME near the edge of town.

Old Jake's home had TWO SMALL WINDOWS that let in the light but kept out the cold.

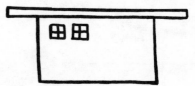

Whereas most of the homes in Kettleville had either stone or brick chimneys, Old Jake's home had A SMALL STOVEPIPE that stuck through the roof. This led down to an old potbelly stove, which kept his little home warm in the winter and on which he cooked all of his meals.

But all the children in Kettleville knew that the most important thing the old potbelly stove was used for was *storytelling*. Why, Old Jake was the very best storyteller the town had ever had! Every Saturday morning, the town's children would go to Old Jake's.

The first thing they would see as they turned down the dirt road on which Old Jake lived was THE SMOKE COMING FROM HIS CHIMNEY. This made them think of the potbelly stove and smile.

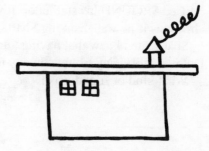

Old Jake would be waiting for them on HIS FRONT PORCH and wave to them as they trudged up the lane to his home.

UP THE STEPS they would bound as each of them gave Old Jake a big hug.

"Let's get on inside and see what Grannie has cooked up for us," he would always say. He called his potbelly stove "Grannie" and all of the children knew that Grannie baked the best cookies in the whole wide world!

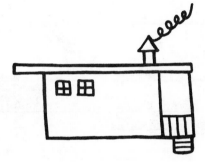

Today, as the children bounded into Old Jake's home, they saw THE BIG OLD COOKIE JAR sitting in the middle of the table.

"Oh goodie," squealed Julie.

"Help yourselves," laughed Old Jake.

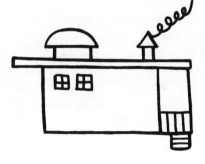

Billy took the lid off the cookie jar and in he reached. He quickly pulled out A RAISIN COOKIE and exclaimed, "Wow!"

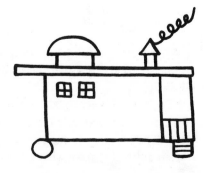

It had ONE LARGE RAISIN RIGHT IN THE MIDDLE.

Julie, Sandy, and Nick each PULLED OUT A COOKIE for themselves.

They were all the same, EACH WITH A BIG RAISIN IN ITS CENTER.

After the last cookie had disappeared, the children gathered around the potbelly stove and waited for Old Jake to begin his story.

"The story I want to tell you young'uns today is about the 'TALL L' RAILROAD LINE I used to work for. I call the story 'The Mystery in the Red _____ .' "

Can anybody guess what Old Jake's mystery was about?

Where's Lucinda?

Beula Beetle and Florence Fly had been waiting a long time for their friend Lucinda. They were going to their favorite spot—THE HAPPY U CAMPGROUNDS. People were always leaving such wonderful treats, such as strawberry jam on bits of bread and cake crumbs.

"Where on earth do you think our friend Lucinda is?" said Beula.

"She is never late," said Florence. "Maybe something has happened to her."

"Well, we had better go look," said Beula.

So the two friends decided to go looking for Lucinda. First they FLEW TOGETHER TO LUCINDA'S HOME, but she was not there.

Then they decided to each fly in different directions and meet at the Happy U Campgrounds. So BEULA FLEW THIS WAY. . .

. . . AND FLORENCE FLEW THIS WAY. But when they met at the campgrounds, neither one of them had seen Lucinda. They were really beginning to worry now.

"Where could she be?" asked Beula.

"Oh, I just know something awful has happened to her," moaned Florence.

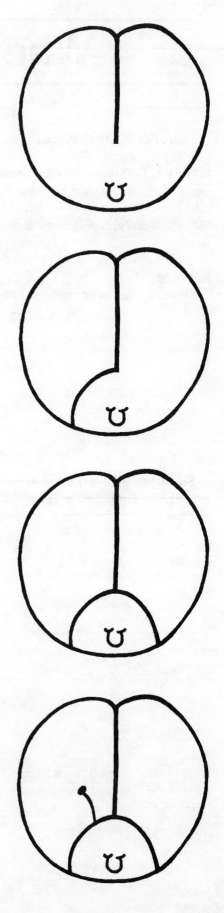

"I know," said Beula. "Let's go to the top of McGregor's Hill. We can see for miles up there."

So that is what they did. Beula WENT UP THIS SIDE OF THE HILL . . .

. . . and Florence WENT UP THE OTHER SIDE OF THE HILL. But when they got there, they had still not found Lucinda!

But they were not going to give up. They decided to each climb up the highest trees on the hilltop and see if they could find their friend. So FLORENCE CLIMBED UP THIS TREE . . .

... AND BEULA CLIMBED UP THIS ONE. From high up in these trees, the bugs could see all the way back to the Happy U Campgrounds.

"Do you see her?" shouted Florence.

"No," yelled Beula. "Let's go back to the campgrounds. Maybe we missed her there."

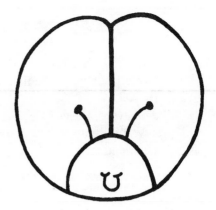

So the two bugs flew back to the Happy U Campgrounds. As they flew into the campgrounds, they each saw TWO PAPER PLATES some campers must have left.

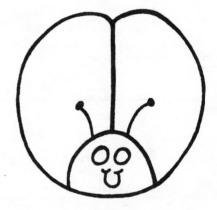

They knew they could usually find some very tasty tidbits on paper plates, SO BEULA FLEW DOWN TO THIS ONE . . .

. . . AND FLORENCE FLEW DOWN TO THE OTHER ONE.

They were just about to begin eating when they heard Lucinda's voice.

"Where have you been? I've been looking everywhere for you."

Florence and Beula both turned to see their friend. What do you think their friend is?

The Leptude Lizard

Victoria Smelts' third grade class was ready to begin their first field trip of the year. This wasn't the normal trip, but Ms. Smelts wasn't a normal teacher. The "Smelters," as Ms. S liked to call them, were in search of the lost Leptude Lizard—a creature many believed to be a fierce relative of the extinct dinosaurs! They began their trip HERE in the Leptudian Jungle.

The Smelters hadn't learned much about exploring yet and ended up going in CIRCLES much of the first day.

On day two, Ms. S suggested they FOLLOW THE ZONMOAM RIVER, since the Leptude Lizard was known to sunbathe along the banks.

The Smelters hadn't learned much about keeping track of supplies, either, and forgot to bring their cameras. The Leptude Lizard, if still alive, had to be photographed. So Ms. S led the class over a rope bridge and BACK TOWARDS CAMP.

23

The Smelters also hadn't learned much about reading a compass, and were soon lost in the jungle. They narrowly escaped danger as they WALKED ALONG THE EDGE OF A POINTED CLIFF.

Back on solid land, the Smelters CONTINUED their hike, always on the lookout for Leptude Lizard tracks as well as their camp.

They found the tracks first—a complete set of FOOTPRINTS! All of them looked the same, with three dangerous-looking nails on the end of each foot.

The Smelters continued in silence, on the lookout for Leptude Lizard. THEY CAREFULLY FOLLOWED the tracks, which seemed to be going in the direction of their camp.

The Smelters still hadn't learned much about tracking, for they found themselves TRAPPED IN A NARROW OPENING between two cliffs. There was only one way out—and that was right where the Leptude Lizard tracks stopped!

Soon they saw it! They thought at first they were all doomed—mere victims of the Leptude Lizard! Its teeth flashed brightly, ROWS AND ROWS OF SHINY WHITE SPIKES. They all stood silently, frozen in terror.

After a bit of staring, Ms. S told the class not to worry. The Leptude Lizard was simply a common jungle reptile. And if her calculations were correct, this particular reptile should begin napping in the afternoon sun right about now.

The Smelters were amazed. Ms. S was right. Leptude Lizard or not, the creature yawned, laid down, and slept. The Smelters carefully crept about from between the cliffs and RAN RIGHT INTO CAMP. What luck!

Solving the mystery of the Leptude Lizard was fun, but the Smelters thought they'd like a little less adventure the next time. The next time, reported a weary Ms. S, would be a trip to the local post office. The children applauded wildly.

What was the Leptude Lizard?

Come Over and See My New Pet

Greg was so excited—his parents had just bought him a new pet! He could hardly wait to show his friend Mike. HE RAN AS FAST AS HE COULD TO MIKE'S HOME.

Mike lived in a home at a place they called THREE FORKS. This was because three roads all came together at this point.

"Hi, Mike," Greg said, "guess what? I have a new pet! Want to come and see what it is?"

"Sure," said Mike. "But I have to finish washing the dishes first."

"I'll help so we can get done sooner," said Greg.

Actually, Mike was almost finished. Greg grabbed a towel and first DRIED A BOWL.

Then he dried TWO FORKS.

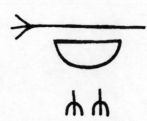

Finally he picked up A DISH TO DRY IT, BUT
THERE WAS STILL SOME FOOD ON IT.

"You'll have to wash this dirty dish over again," said
Greg.

"Oh, hooey . . . I would just wipe that little bit off
with the towel. You sure are picky!"

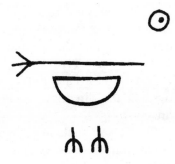

Both boys laughed as Mike quickly washed off the
spot of food from the dish. They hung up the wet towels
and started for the door.

"I'm going over to Greg's," hollered Mike.

"Oh, Mike. I have A BIG PLATE OF COOKIES I
wish you would take to Grandma's on your way to
Greg's house."

So before the boys went to Greg's home, they had to
go to Mike's Grandma's house, which meant they had to
GO AROUND THE BLOCK.

Just as they were going up Greg's driveway, his dad called from the garage. As the boys entered the garage, Greg's dad said, "Hi, Mike! Say, Greg, I need your help. I'm trying to cut THIS HEAVY WIRE WITH THESE WIRE CUTTERS and I'm having trouble. Will you boys hold the wire for me so I can use both hands on the wire cutters?"

"Sure, Dad," said Greg. "What are you making?"

"Oh, you'll see soon enough. It's something for your new pet."

As soon as the wire was cut, the boys ran into the house. Before they entered the living room, they heard a loud "Squawk!"

Can you guess what Greg's new pet is?

Silver Blades

Melissa was not happy. Her annual Ice Skating Show at the local rink was about to open and Uncle Harry had not yet arrived.

"He's never missed a show," Melissa said to her mother.

"Be patient," said her mother.

"He'll make it if he can," added her father. "Business has been good, and it's not easy for him to get away."

"I hope he makes it," said a worried Melissa as she put her aching, TIRED FEET UPON THE COFFEE TABLE.

"Melissa," her mother sighed, "get your feet off the furniture and come help set the table."

"Can't have Harry welcomed with an empty table," laughed Papa as he stirred the soup.

That was all the encouragement Melissa needed. She quickly RAN AROUND THE TABLE placing forks, spoons, and knives to make the table ready for Uncle Harry.

Almost crazy trying to wait quietly for her uncle, Melissa decided to lace up her skates and PRACTICE HER SCHOOL FIGURES for the Ice Show.

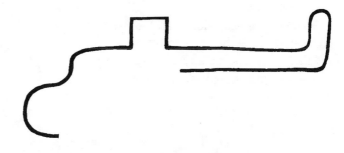

Uncle Harry always told Melissa of her great improvement from year to year. She surely didn't want to let him down. The snow began to fall as she silently GLIDED ALONG on top of the frozen pond.

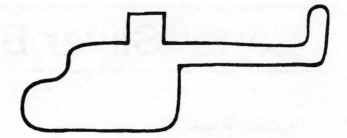

The silence was broken as Melissa's blade caught on a frozen twig and sent her stumbling down the pond.

"These dumb old skates," mumbled Melissa.

She looked down at the ROUGH BLADES. One more season of skating and Papa said she could then have a new pair.

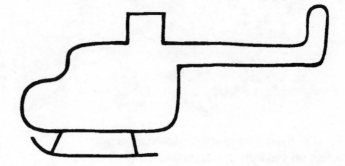

The sky began to turn a purple gray. Soon she would have to give up on Uncle Harry coming at all. Sadly, she pushed off to practice her FIGURE EIGHTS.

Just then a noise louder than Melissa had ever heard shook the sky. Melissa looked up and there was Uncle Harry, holding new skates! Delighted, Melissa knew this would be the best Ice Show ever.

How did Uncle Harry arrive in time for Melissa's Ice Show?

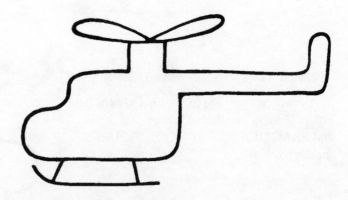

Another Story, Grandpa, Please

The year was 2089 and the twins had decided that *this* year was the year they learned the truth about Grandpa. Having looked everywhere else in the house, they reluctantly agreed to try the attic. They slowly CLIMBED THE NARROW STAIRCASE that took them to the top of Grandpa's grand old home.

As they pushed open the heavy wooden door, its hinges creaked with old age and years of poor care. They might have stopped then, but their mission of finding out what Grandpa did when he was a young man made them go on. They put their fears aside and continued with their mission. They carefully LOOKED AROUND THE DOOR into the dimly lit room.

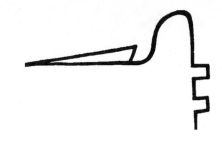

The musty room was completely empty except for TWO OLD TRUNKS sitting patiently on the dusty attic floor.

The twins were very bright and they immediately thought the trunks might contain the answers to all their questions about Grandpa's mysterious career. They opened the first trunk. With a squeal their Grandma's cat Katy JUMPED OUT AND RAN THROUGH THE ATTIC DOOR. She barely touched the ground as she scampered for safety.

Startled, even afraid, the twins more carefully opened the second trunk. They pulled out a photo album and then WALKED OVER TO THE ATTIC WINDOW so as to better look at it. The twins were pleasantly surprised because the album had Grandpa's initials on the cover.

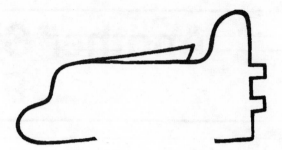

As the twins anxiously looked through the book, they imagined all kinds of exciting careers for their Grandpa. Then they found it—the picture that told all! The twins grabbed the book and RAN DOWN THE STAIRS . . .

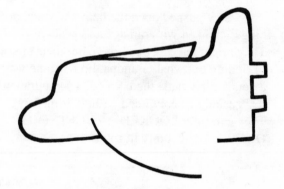

. . . and INTO THE FAMILY ROOM so Grandpa could tell them all the wonderful stories of his exciting life.

What was Grandpa's exciting career?

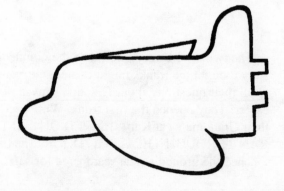

County Fair

Neil and Bill were terribly excited as they neared the fairgrounds. Today was the opening day of the Hancock County Fair and they were going to spend the entire day at the fair! As they neared the fairgrounds, they saw THE HUGE ARCH over the main entrance.

Neil and Bill bought their tickets and HURRIED THROUGH THE ARCH.

As soon as they entered the fair, they heard someone yell, "Hey, Bill! Hey, Neil!"

They both looked up to see TWO OF THEIR FRIENDS from school, Greg and Pete.

"Hey, guys," said Greg as the four friends hurried toward one another. "Pete and I were just going to ride on the Sky Dip. Want to go with us?"

"If you're not afraid," added Pete with a grin.

"Afraid!" said Bill. "Let's go on it now!"

So the four friends bought their tickets and got in the small car. Slowly it took them UP A STEEP INCLINE.

Once it reached the top, the four friends were very quiet and held tightly to the handrail. The car then RACED TO THE GROUND with everyone yelling and laughing.

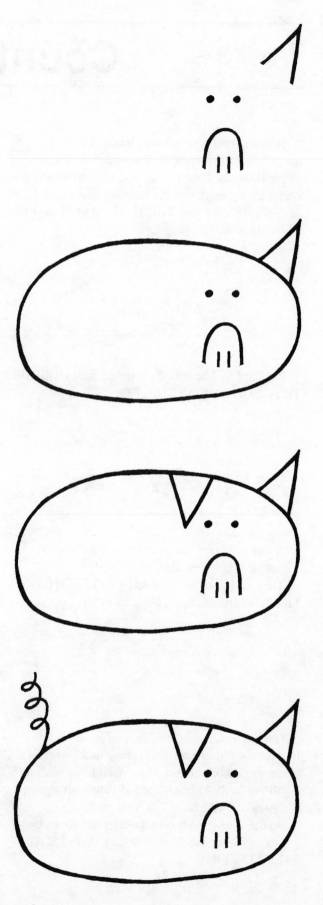

"Let's go to the racetrack and see what's happening there," said Neil, as soon as the boys had gotten off the Sky Dip.

"Yeah," they all agreed, and walked over to the racetrack. It was A LARGE QUARTER-MILE RACETRACK.

The boys arrived just in time to see a group of horses lining up at the starting gates. In no time at all, the starter DROPPED HIS FLAG and the race began.

It was an exciting race and a horse named Bolt of Lightning won by a head. One lady got so excited that she let go of the balloon she was holding for her little girl. The wind caught it and it was carried HIGH ABOVE THE FAIRGROUNDS.

The boys were walking back to the midway as they passed a large building.

"What do you think is in there?" asked Bill.

"Let's go in and see," said Greg.

When they entered the building, their ears were filled with a chorus of animal sounds. All of the prize-winning animals seemed to be in this building. They walked past stall after stall until Pete said, "Wow—look at that! Penelope won FOUR FIRST PLACE RIBBONS!"

"Gosh," said Neil WITH A BIG SMILE, "Penelope belongs to my Uncle John. I bet he sure is proud!"

Now what do you think Penelope is?

Mirror on the Palace Wall

A long time ago, in a land closer than you might think, lived an old king. His kingdom was large and his castle was large. Even he was large—and quite proud of it! Unfortunately, this king had a favorite story of a girl whose beauty was above all others. This girl had a stepmother who checked her own beauty in a mirror. One day, the king had an idea. The king decided to construct a large, GRAND MIRROR in his palace.

The king called to his mirror: "Mirror on the palace wall, who is the largest of them all?"

The mirror gave an answer, but it wasn't the king who was the largest! The king was furious! He couldn't believe it!

"Build me another mirror," he ordered. AND SO IT WAS DONE.

The king called to his second mirror: "Mirror on the palace wall, who is the largest of them all?"

The mirror could only speak the truth, and gave the same answer as the first. The king was outraged! He ordered ANOTHER MIRROR—and when it was done, it gave the very same answer!

The king ordered yet ANOTHER MIRROR and *still* came the same answer to his question!

The king was at his wits' end. "Surely I am the grandest, largest thing in my entire large kingdom. I cannot accept the mirrors' answer."

With that, he set to pacing up and down the winding palace staircase. UP AND DOWN HE WENT—pacing and thinking, thinking and pacing some more.

Finally, he had a solution. "Bring me the largest mirror in all of my kingdom," he cried.

When the massive MIRROR WAS DELIVERED and the king asked his question, the same old answer was given. The king was horrified.

After weeks of thinking, the king decided to build the LARGEST MIRROR IN ALL THE WORLD! The cost was outrageous and left the king penniless, but he had to hear that he was the largest and most powerful creature in his kingdom!

When the mirror was delivered, the king STOOD IN FRONT OF HIS REFLECTION and asked, "Largest mirror on the wall, who is the largest of them all?"

The mirror hesitated and then gave the same answer as always. The king, heartbroken and penniless, left the palace weeping and was never heard from again.

The answer to his question, always true, is now right in front of you!

Planet U

Security Spaceship was hurtling through space. It was one of the oldest spaceships still in use and resembled A ROCKET.

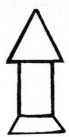

The crew of Security Spaceship was on a mission to PLANET U. This was a newly discovered planet and the crew had orders to investigate it in order to see if any form of life might be found.

In order to reach Planet U, the crew had to navigate their old spaceship between the TWIN PLANETS.

Just as Security Spaceship was passing the twin planets, a shower of meteors passed them. ONE LARGE METEOR shot by on this side of the spaceship . . .

. . . and ANOTHER LARGE ONE passed close by on the other side.

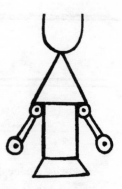

Soon the crew carefully landed their spaceship on A FLAT SURFACE of Planet U.

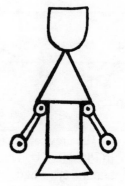

Through their television monitors, they saw A LONE MOUNTAIN PEAK in the distance. Other than that, all of the surface seemed flat. They were glad, as that would make their investigation that much easier.

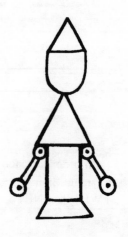

The captain decided that it would be quicker if the crew was divided into two teams. Each team would then search the planet in opposite directions. ONE TEAM WENT TO THE EAST OF THE PLANET . . .

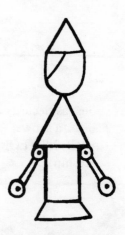

. . . AND SET UP CAMP HERE.

The other team WENT WEST . . .

. . . AND SET UP CAMP HERE.

Early the next morning they each broke camp and
MADE THEIR WAYS TOWARD ONE ANOTHER
until they met near the center of the mysterious
planet.

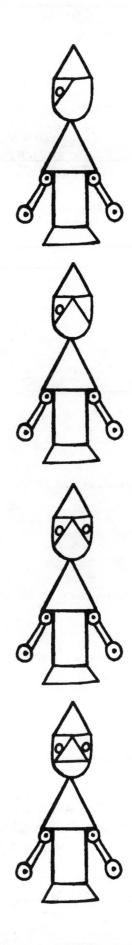

They decided it would be impossible to search the southern portion of the planet, as it was TOO DARK.

Therefore, they made their way BACK TO THE SPACESHIP.

When they arrived back at Security Spaceship, one of the crew members yelled, "Look over there!" He was pointing at one of the spaceship's wings. TWO LARGE EYES were peering out from under it.

What do you think the crew found on the other side of their spaceship?

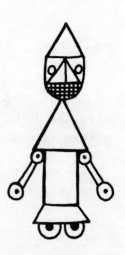

Daniel's Incredible Adventure

If you asked Daniel how he liked being a dolphin, he would tell you it was just fine. Now, he was only six months old, so being a dolphin was pretty new. Except for the occasional shark, however, his life was full of sunny, happy days.

One day, not so long ago, as Daniel was JUMPING IN AND OUT OF THE CLEAR WATER, he saw something he'd not seen before. He immediately dove back into the sea and swam for home.

"Mother, Mother," cried a concerned Daniel.
"What now, dear?" replied a very busy mother.
Daniel began to explain what he had seen. "It HAD A FIN, Mother, just like a shark."
"But it wasn't a shark, dear?" asked his mother.
"No," answered a confused Daniel.

"And it wiggled like a STALK OF SEAWEED," added Daniel.
"But it wasn't seaweed?" asked his mother.
"No," replied Daniel

"I see," said Mother. "Anything else you remember?"

"Well," thought Daniel, "on top of its head it had a BIRD'S BEAK."

"But it wasn't a bird?"

"Right!" said Daniel.

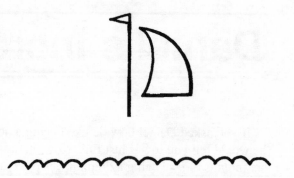

"And how did this thing move, Daniel?" asked Mother.

"In a STRAIGHT LINE at first—as straight and long as an eel."

"At first?" questioned his mother.

"Yes ma'am, then it turned. Not slow and bending like an angelfish, but more like a minnow—quick and sharp. And then IT HEADED IN THE OTHER DIRECTION."

"I see," said Mother.

"Perhaps I'd better have a look," said Mother. "Can you remember where you saw this strange creature?"

"I think so," said a proud Daniel. "Follow me."

And off they went through the sea past coral reefs and quiet clams. Their journey was LONG, but they finally reached the spot.

"This it it, Mother," said Daniel.

"Very well," replied Mother. "Let's surface and take a look."

So Daniel SURFACED HERE . . .

. . . and his Mother SURFACED HERE.

"Oh, Daniel!" laughed Mother. "This is your creature? I can see there are still many things you need to learn!"

As they swam toward home, Daniel's mother told him of many things.

The Great White Lion

Members of the Voi Safari were terribly excited. They had just received news that the Great White Lion had been seen in the region of the twin lakes. They had been tracking this lion for over a week and now felt very close to seeing him. This region was named Twin Lakes because of TWO LAKES that were not only the same size and shape . . .

. . . but each had a similar SMALL ISLAND IN ITS CENTER.

Once the Voi Safari reached the twin lakes region, the members proceeded to SET UP THEIR CAMP.

The campsite was on a small flat plain and ALMOST COMPLETELY SURROUNDED BY TALL GRASS. It was dark by the time the tents were assembled, and so the tired hunters went straight to bed.

Early the next morning, they left camp and began MAKING THEIR WAY AROUND ONE OF THE LAKES, keeping a watchful eye for any sign of the Great White Lion.

By noon they were halfway around this lake and they still had not spotted the Great White Lion. So after they had eaten lunch, they decided TO DIG A LARGE PIT in which to capture the lion. It was their hope that the lion would be tempted by the meat they were leaving and unexpectedly fall into the pit.

When the pit was completed, they continued the hunt, slowly MAKING THEIR WAY BACK TOWARD THEIR CAMPSITE.

But they soon came to A SMALL RIVER. Fortunately, it was not deep, and they were able to wade across to the other side.

After crossing the river, THEY FINALLY REACHED THEIR CAMP. It had been a very hard day and they were all exhausted. So they quickly ate their meal and went straight to bed, since they would continue their hunt early the next morning.

When they awoke, the sky was filled with DARK RAIN CLOUDS. Many of the hunters thought they should stay around camp that day, but the safari leader laughed and said, "Stay here if you want. I am going to find the Great White Lion!"

So they all decided to go with the leader and soon were MAKING THEIR WAY AROUND THE OTHER LAKE.

Once they reached the other side of the lake, they dug ANOTHER DEEP PIT, again hoping to capture the lion.

When the pit was finished, they continued their hunt, MAKING THEIR WAY BACK TOWARD THE CAMPSITE . . .

. . . until, once again, they came to that same SMALL RIVER.

After crossing the river, they QUICKLY MADE THEIR WAY BACK TO THEIR CAMP, as it was beginning to rain.

The hunters were thoroughly drenched as they made their way into camp, so they built A LARGE FIRE in the center of their campsite in order to warm and dry themselves.

The next day was the final day of the safari. The hunters went back to the pits they had dug, but they were both empty. They were really disappointed and the leader told them that the Great White Lion was probably a long way from the Twin Lake area by now.

As the Voi Safari left the region to return to their homes, they frightened A LARGE BIRD THAT SLOWLY FLEW AWAY OVER THE TWIN LAKES.

Now what do you think? Do you think the leader was right, or do you think the Great White Lion was simply hiding?

School Can Be an Adventure?

It was going to be another boring year of reading, writing, and recess—at least that's what Joan and Carlos thought as they looked at the city map.

"At least it's a new building," Joan said. "It's right here on this map."

Joan DREW A CIRCLE AROUND THE LOCATION AND PUT AN X ON TOP OF THE NEW BUILDING.

Early the next morning, Carlos reluctantly joined Joan. "Cheer up, Buddy!" said Joan as they WALKED TOWARD THE X on the map. "This new building is supposed to be one of a kind, a real fun place in which to learn."

"I've heard that before," sighed Carlos.

As the school came into view, Joan had to agree with Carlos. "I guess you're right, FOUR WALLS AND A ROOF aren't very exciting," she said.

"Well, we're already here," said Carlos. "Let's give it a try."

The two friends walked inside—and were they ever surprised! There were no classrooms, just a big desk with a gray-haired woman behind it.

"Welcome to Ed. C—that's short for Education Central," she chuckled. "You two are going to be tardy if you don't hurry. Now, listen carefully. TAKE A LEFT OUTSIDE, GO DOWN THE LONG WALK, THEN MAKE A RIGHT TURN and you will arrive at your first class. Run along, now." The friends quickly did as they were told.

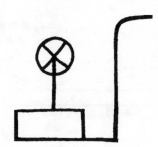

When the two reached the edge of the walk, there was nothing in sight. "I guess we're tardy," said Joan. "We'd better ask that lady at Ed. C what to do now."

As the two STARTED DOWN THE WALK, they saw a group of students.

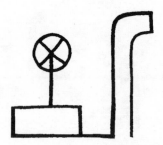

"You two are just in time," shouted the teacher. "Follow us."
AND THEY DID.

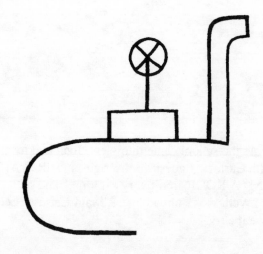

After they had walked quite a way, Carlos finally got up the courage to ask a question. "Excuse me sir, but where are we going?"

"Why, to science class, of course," came the reply from the teacher.

Carlos shrugged his shoulders and CONTINUED FOLLOWING.

Ten minutes later, THE CLASS ARRIVED AT THE VERY SPOT WHERE THEY HAD STARTED. "Here we are," said the teacher. "Science class! Watch your step as you enter the classroom."

Carlos and Joan followed as the class CLIMBED DOWN THROUGH FOUR HOLES beside the walk.

"Today," said the teacher, "we are studying underwater animals. Quickly find a seat and prepare to learn."

Everyone SAT IN PAIRS as they waited for class to begin.

"An ordinary school?" said Joan to Carlos with a smile. "We're about to be in an adventure."

"I don't think this year will be boring after all!" said Carlos.

"Quiet please," added the teacher. "If you will all pull back the curtains and LOOK OUT YOUR WINDOWS, we will begin our adventure and our voyage."

The students did as the teacher said. They were surprised to discover that they were the first students ever to have class in a _____!